PARABLES

Stories of the
Kingdom

A Guided Discovery for Groups and Individuals

Amy Welborn

LOYOLA PRESS.
A JESUIT MINISTRY
Chicago

LOYOLA PRESS.
A JESUIT MINISTRY

3441 N. Ashland Avenue
Chicago, Illinois 60657
(800) 621-1008
www.loyolapress.com

Nihil Obstat	*Imprimatur*
Reverend John Lodge, S.S.L., S.T.D.	Most Reverend Raymond E. Goedert, M.A., S.T.L., J.C.L.
Censor Deputatus	Vicar General
January 5, 2003	Archdiocese of Chicago
	January 9, 2003

The *Nihil Obstat* and *Imprimatur* are official declarations that a book is free of doctrinal and moral error. No implication is contained therein that those who have granted the Nihil Obstat and Imprimatur agree with the content, opinions, or statements expressed. Nor do they assume any legal responsibility associated with publication.

The Scripture quotations contained herein are from the New Revised Standard Version Bible: Catholic Edition, copyright © 1993 and 1989 by the Division of Christian Education of the National Council of the Churches of Christ in the U.S.A. Used by permission. All rights reserved. Subheadings in Scripture quotations have been added by Amy Welborn.

The excerpt from St. Cyprian's Epistle LI (p. 33) can be found in *The Ante-Nicene Fathers*, vol. V, on the Christian Classics Ethereal Library Web site, http://www.ccel.org.

The excerpt from St. Thérèse of Lisieux (p. 43) can be found in John Clarke, O.C.D., trans., *Story of a Soul: The Autobiography of Saint Thérèse of Lisieux* (Washington, D.C.: ICS Publications, 1996), 242. Copyright © 1975, 1976, 1996 by Washington Province of Discalced Carmelites, ICS Publications, 2131 Lincoln Road, N.E., Washington, D.C. 20002-1199, U.S.A., http://www.icspublications.org. Used with permission.

The prayer of Cardinal John Henry Newman, adapted by Mother Teresa (p. 52), can be found at the Missionaries of Charity Third Order Web site, http://www.mciiio.org/prayer.html.

The excerpt from Cardinal John Henry Newman's sermon "Promising without Doing" (p. 53) can be found in *Parochial and Plain Sermons* (San Francisco: Ignatius Press, 1987), 106; also at http://www.newmanreader.org/works/parochial/volume1/sermon13.html.

The excerpt from St. Benedict's Rule (p. 63) can be found in Dwight Longnecker, *Listen, My Son: St. Benedict for Fathers* (Harrisburg, Pa.: Morehouse Publications, 2000), 221. Translation by Abbot Parry, O.S.B.

The excerpt from St. Teresa of Ávila's "For the Veiling of Sister Isabel De Los Angeles" (p. 73) can be found in Kieran Kavanaugh and Otilio Rodriguez, trans., *The Collected Works of St. Teresa of Avila*, vol. 3 (Washington, D.C.: ICS Publications, 1980). Copyright © 1980 by Washington Province of Discalced Carmelites, ICS Publications, 2131 Lincoln Road, N.E., Washington, D.C. 20002-1199, U.S.A., http://www.icspublications.org. Used with permission.

Interior design by Kay Hartmann/Communique Design
Illustration by Charise Mericle Harper

ISBN-13: 978-0-8294-1472-1
ISBN-10: 0-8294-1472-X

Printed in the United States of America
12 13 14 15 16 17 18 Bang 10 9 8 7 6 5 4

Contents

4   *How to Use This Guide*

6   *Why Do You Speak to Them in Parables?*

14 **Week 1**
Ready to Listen?
Mark 4:1–20

24 **Week 2**
A Merciful God
Matthew 20:1–16; Luke 15:1–10

34 **Week 3**
How to Pray
Luke 11:5–10; 18:1–14

44 **Week 4**
Which of These?
Matthew 21:28–32; Luke 10:25–37

54 **Week 5**
God Calls
Matthew 25:14–30; Luke 14:15–24

64 **Week 6**
Awake for the Lord
Luke 12:35–48; Matthew 25:1–13

74 *When Will Jesus Return?*

76 *Suggestions for Bible Discussion Groups*

79 *Suggestions for Individuals*

80 *Resources*

How to Use This Guide

You might compare the Bible to a national park. The park is so large that you could spend months, even years, getting to know it. But a brief visit, if carefully planned, can be enjoyable and worthwhile. In a few hours you can drive through the park and pull over at a handful of sites. At each stop you can get out of the car, take a short trail through the woods, listen to the wind blowing through the trees, get a feel for the place.

In this booklet we will read some of the parables of Jesus that were recorded in the Gospels. The Bible contains more parables than we will have an opportunity to study, but those that have been selected will give you a good introduction to the style and purpose of Jesus' parables in general.

This guide provides everything you need to explore the parables in six discussions—or to do a six-part exploration on your own. The introduction on page 6 will prepare you to get the most out of your reading. The weekly sections provide cultural and religious background information on the parables and on those who listened to them. Equally important, each section supplies questions that will launch your group into fruitful discussion, helping you to both investigate the parables for yourself and learn from one another. If you're using the booklet by yourself, the questions will spur your personal reflection.

Each discussion is meant to be a *guided discovery*.

Guided. None of us is equipped to read the Bible without help. We read the Bible *for* ourselves but not *by* ourselves. Scripture was written to be understood and applied in the community of faith. So each week "A Guide to the Reading," drawing on the work of both modern biblical scholars and Christian writers of the past, supplies background and explanations. The guide will help you grasp the message of the parables. Think of it as a friendly park ranger who points out noteworthy details and explains what you're looking at so you can appreciate things for yourself.

Discovery. The purpose is for *you* to interact with these parables that Jesus told. "Questions for Careful Reading" is a tool to help you dig into the text and examine it carefully. "Questions for

Application" will help you consider what these words mean for your life here and now. Each week concludes with an "Approach to Prayer" section that helps you respond to God's word. Supplementary "Living Tradition" and "Saints in the Making" sections offer the thoughts and experiences of Christians past and present. By showing what the parables have meant to others, these sections will help you consider what they mean for you.

How long are the discussion sessions? We've assumed you will have about an hour and a half when you get together. If you have less time, you'll find that most of the elements can be shortened somewhat.

Is homework necessary? You will get the most out of your discussions if you read the weekly material and prepare the answers to the questions in advance of each meeting. If participants are not able to prepare, have someone read the "Guide to the Reading" sections aloud to the group at the points where they appear.

What about leadership? If you happen to have a world-class biblical scholar in your group, by all means ask him or her to lead the discussions. In the absence of any professional Scripture scholars, or even accomplished amateur biblical scholars, you can still have a first-class Bible discussion. Choose two or three people to take turns as facilitators, and have everyone read "Suggestions for Bible Discussion Groups" (page 76) before beginning.

Does everyone need a guide? a Bible? Everyone in the group will need his or her own copy of this booklet. It contains the entire text of every parable discussed, so a Bible is not absolutely necessary—but each participant will find it useful to have one. You should have at least one Bible on hand for your discussions. (See page 80 for recommendations.)

How do we get started? Before you begin, take a look at the suggestions for Bible discussion groups (page 76) or individuals (page 79).

Why Do You Speak to Them in Parables?

When we think of the ministry of Jesus, we probably think of great miracles and small moments of grace. We think of shared meals, healed bodies, and grateful, forgiven hearts.

We probably think of parables as well.

Jesus taught his disciples and the crowds that followed him in both actions and words. Sometimes he spoke in simple statements—"Blessed are the poor"—and at other times he issued warnings. Stern ones too, mostly to religious leaders: "Woe to you Pharisees . . ." At other times—a great many other times—he told stories. Not just any kind of stories, mind you, not anecdotes, epics, or fables. What Jesus told were parables.

The word *parable* is derived from a Greek word that means "comparison." We call Jesus' stories parables because they invite us to see a comparison: between the kingdom of God and a banquet, between God and a landowner, between ourselves and . . . which are we, anyway? The Pharisee or the tax collector? The older son or the younger? The bridesmaids who are prepared or those who are caught short? The workers who toil all day or the latecomers?

If you are already familiar with these parables, your response to those questions might well be different today than it was five or ten years ago. That is because Jesus' parables, like the rest of God's word, are living words. They speak to us now in a different way than they did in the past. The way we hear them changes as our lives change and as our understanding of life deepens. Jesus told the parables to crowds gathered in Palestine hundreds of years ago. But he also tells them to us, *today*. Our willingness to clear away the obstacles to heartfelt, open listening to their message for us will determine how fruitful our reading of the parables will be.

A simple question before we begin our readings: What kind of stories are Jesus' parables? They are not literary short stories like those we read in anthologies or magazines. Short stories give attention to plot and character development. Jesus' parables are rarely longer than a couple hundred words, and the motives of the characters are often not explained at all. Why, for example, would a landowner hire workers throughout the day rather than hiring all he needed in the morning? Was he so shortsighted that he failed to gauge how many workers he would need and found himself having to hire more during the day? Jesus doesn't explain the landowner's odd behavior. His motive, it seems, is not important. Something else must be, but what?

Jesus' parables are not fables either. We are all familiar with Aesop's fables, such as the race of the tortoise and the hare, in which the characters are often animals and the narrative ends with an enlightening or cautionary lesson. We might be tempted to place Jesus' parables in the same category: short tales with a moral at the end. Jesus, however, doesn't tell stories about animals. And besides, his stories are not always constructed as narratives that provide an obvious moral. Often Jesus does not explain his stories at all, much less provide an easily understood lesson. If Jesus doesn't provide us with an application, how are we to respond? If the moral isn't the key to understanding Jesus' parables, what is?

The point of Jesus' parables, as the name implies, is the comparison. In listening to a parable, we are invited to perceive the God we cannot see through a comparison of him and his ways with that which we can see. Jesus compares and then invites us to compare. He calls us not just to listen but also to respond to his invitation to encounter—right here, right now—the reality of God and his reign over human beings.

Jesus was not the first Jewish teacher to tell parables. As was the case with much of his ministry, he drew on a tradition that was familiar to his hearers and transformed it into something new.

In the Old Testament, we find about ten stories that are similar to Jesus' parables. One of the most famous is the story that the prophet Nathan told to King David (2 Samuel 12:1–4). David, the great king of Israel, fell in love with Bathsheba, the wife of Uriah, an officer in his army. In order to have Bathsheba to himself, David had Uriah sent to make a foolhardy attack on the enemy so that he would be killed, and he was.

Nathan was David's chief spiritual adviser. Hearing of David's act, Nathan entered David's court and told him about a wealthy man who had stolen a poor man's only sheep. After telling the story, Nathan asked David what should be done about such an act. David, enraged, said that the wealthy man should be killed. His rage turned to grief and repentance when Nathan told him, "You are the man!" David realized that his taking Bathsheba was like the wealthy man's theft of the poor man's sheep. The comparison—the parable—shocked him into a realization of his sin.

Rabbis who lived in the period during and after Jesus' time also told parables. Many feature a king, who almost always represents God, and refer to God's kingdom. Characters often behave in unusual ways, and some of the language used in these parables is similar to Jesus' way of speaking—for example, the use of introductory formulas such as "To what shall we compare . . ." and a phrase indicating the conclusion, "thus it is . . ." Even if you're only slightly familiar with Jesus' parables, you can see some similarities. Some of Jesus' parables feature a king who represents God. Characters sometimes behave strangely, such as the master who pays all of his workers the same wage no matter what time of the day they began their labor (Matthew 20:1–16).

But there is an important difference between Jesus' parables and those of the rabbis. The parables told by the rabbis most often illustrated a point in Scripture. These parables were usually tied into a broader argument. Although Jesus' parables are obviously tied into his broader message about God's kingdom and our place in it, their purpose is not exactly that of an anecdote inserted in a larger discussion to illustrate certain points. Jesus' parables are not designed to reinforce interpretations of Scripture. Jesus tells parables in specific situations. Sometimes they are responses to specific questions. On occasion, Jesus directs a parable to a particular person—as Nathan hurled his parable at David. Thus while Jesus' parables contain lessons, they are more than that. Jesus spoke directly to his first followers with his parables, and through them he continues to address us directly today. As we encounter the parables, we are challenged to a deeper kind of listening, a listening in which we allow ourselves to be confronted by Jesus' words in the present.

But why parables? Why doesn't Jesus simply speak directly, without the comparisons of parables? Why doesn't he present his message about God's kingdom in a more straightforward way and tell us how we should respond to it? Why these stories?

If we ask this question, we're not alone. The Gospels tell us that the disciples asked this very question of Jesus, as we will see in our reading in week 1. There we will examine the question more closely, but it is helpful to cite Jesus' words now, right up front, so we are attuned to Jesus' approach from the beginning.

Why, his disciples asked Jesus, was he instructing the crowd in parables? The question implies that he did not use parables in his conversations with the disciples. They were understandably puzzled by this. Jesus answered: "To you it has been given to know the secrets of the kingdom of heaven, but to them it has not been given.-.-.-. The reason I speak to them in parables is that 'seeing they do not perceive, and hearing they do not listen, nor do they understand'" (Matthew 13:11, 13).

We may easily feel frustrated by Jesus' explanation. What on earth could he mean? He tells stories because we are spiritually blind? But the parables are so confusing at times. How could they help to clarify things?

Our bafflement may only get worse when we turn to Mark's version of Jesus' words in this incident: "For those outside, everything comes in parables; *in order that* 'they may indeed look, but not perceive, and may indeed listen, but not understand; so that they may not turn again and be forgiven'" (Mark 4:11–12, emphasis added). Now, this is really distressing. Is Jesus saying that he speaks in parables because he *wants* to confuse us and direct us away from, instead of toward, the truth? How could that be?

There is no easy way of interpreting Jesus' answer to his disciples. The passage in Mark in particular is one of the most discussed verses in the Bible. We will come back to and consider his words in more depth in week 1. But for now, perhaps you are experiencing a vague disorientation, a creeping impression that all is not what you believed it to be—that maybe there's more to these parables and to the Jesus who told them than you thought . . .

Then maybe you're ready to start reading, thinking about, and talking about Jesus' parables! For that feeling of disturbance and perplexity is exactly what Jesus' parables are intended to provoke. They often leave us wondering if all is really as it seems to be. That moment when we start wondering is the moment when our eyes become uncomfortably opened to perceive something beyond the familiar, to catch a glimpse of the God who never runs out of surprises.

The parables in this study guide are found in the Gospels of Matthew, Mark, or Luke. None of them are from the Gospel of John. The reason? Although there are comparisons in John—Jesus compares himself to a vine, a door, and a shepherd—there are no narrative parables in his Gospel. Scholars debate the reasons for this, and since John didn't care to leave an explanation behind, we can be certain that the debate will continue for a very long time.

While some parables that we will read are found in only one or two of the Gospels, many are found in all of the first three Gospels—Matthew, Mark, and Luke. These three Gospels are sometimes called the synoptic Gospels. *Synoptic* is from a Greek word that means "seeing together." These three Gospels have so many parallels that it is possible to set them side by side and look at them together, comparing the episodes in them with one another. The term *synoptic Gospels* is a bit technical, but it is so convenient that we will sometimes use it in our discussions.

If you choose to enter the study of the parables more deeply, you will also find that there are sometimes differences between the versions of the parables in the synoptic Gospels. The parable of the sower, for example, is found in all three synoptic Gospels, and each version is slightly different. How are we to understand these differences?

First, it is possible, even likely, that in the course of his teaching Jesus used each parable more than once and gave it slightly different twists and details for various audiences. That is what any good speaker would do. Thus, some of the differences may have originated with Jesus himself.

Second, some differences in the parables would have arisen as Jesus' disciples told and retold them after his death and resurrection. These earliest Christian teachers probably adapted their accounts to the particular groups of people to whom they preached in order to bring out the message most effectively for each group. Thus, some of the differences arose during the period of oral tradition between Jesus' resurrection and the Gospel writers' composition of the Gospels—a period that probably lasted thirty years or more.

Third, the Gospel writers themselves revised the oral and written material that came to them. Most scholars think that some of the variations between the synoptics are the work of the evangelists themselves, as one Gospel writer drew on the work of another. The most widely held theory is that Mark wrote first and Matthew and Luke, probably unknown to each other, used Mark's Gospel as a source for their own. What was the basis of the changes Matthew and Luke made? To some extent they may have been guided by the variant traditions that were available to them. At points, they may have wished to convey the parable in a form that would have been more easily comprehensible to their particular readers.

Throughout the process of teaching and writing about Jesus, the Holy Spirit was at work. The Spirit guided Jesus' disciples to understand him better after his resurrection than they had been able to do before. Their subsequent experience of Christian life in the Spirit probably helped them see more clearly the importance of certain elements of Jesus' parables. The Gospel writers had the special help of the Spirit as they composed their accounts of Jesus. The writing of the Gospels was a complex and in some ways mysterious process. But we can be confident that the resulting four portraits of Jesus are historically authentic and convey Jesus' teaching in a way that is consistent with his intentions.

We face challenges to understanding Jesus' parables and grasping their message for us. One problem is familiarity. Many of us have heard Jesus' parables since we were children. We have a tendency to zone out as soon as we hear the well-worn introductions: "A sower went out to sow . . . ," "A man went down from Jerusalem to Jericho . . ." Ah yes, we think. Some seed will grow; some will not. The man will be robbed; the hated one will assist him. Be good soil, be tolerant, be helpful. We've got it. Next story, please.

They look but do not see. They hear but do not listen.

How can we be sure that our eyes and ears are indeed open to the living word in Jesus' parables, not dulled by familiarity?

A couple of tactics may be of use.

First, it is helpful to try to make a fresh attempt to see the parables against their cultural background. We don't need to become scholars in the history and sociology of ancient Palestine, but it is useful to learn a little about the world in which Jesus delivered his parables in order to get an idea of how the parables might have sounded to the people who lived in that world. Thus this guide will offer some background information, not to weigh us down with historical data but to help us hear Jesus' words with more clarity and with an appreciation of the sometimes startling effect they had on his first listeners.

Second, as we read and listen to the parables, it is crucial to keep God himself at the center of our thinking. Many of us have a tendency to dilute the parables down to bland, general exhortations to treat other people more kindly. As Christians, we must ask ourselves: If that was all Jesus was up to, why did he bother? Wasn't kindness already covered in Jewish law and tradition?

It was. The Judaism of Jesus' time, which formed his listeners' thinking and behavior, was a deeply compassionate tradition, mindful of God's instructions through the prophets to care for the poor, the widowed, and the orphaned.

So while the right treatment of others is surely an element of the parables of Jesus, often it is not the only point. Jesus is about much more than suggestions for right living. He began his ministry by proclaiming "good news"—and this good news, embodied in Jesus' miracles and vividly illustrated in his parables, is about the activity of God, God's expression of love and mercy. The good news is also about living right, but that right living is not a matter of following abstract rules—it is about responding to the God who is in action now, right here among us, and shaping our lives in relationship to him.

As we go through life, we develop an impression of who God is and expectations for how he will act toward us. Many of our expectations may be solidly grounded in the truth we have been taught and in our own experience, but some are not. Some of our expectations about God flow from ideas we have absorbed from our less-than-Christian culture. Some of our pictures of God may be distorted by negative experiences we have had—negligent or abusive parenting, unanswered prayers, the loss of those we love.

In the parables, Jesus offers a corrective to our mistaken notions. Whenever we find ourselves confused about who God is, how he relates to us, and what he expects from us, it is good to turn to these parables, for in them we find the truth.

When we listen to Jesus' parables, we hear stories told long ago, but told anew to us, this minute. If we pay attention, the ancient images will interact with our own expectations and needs and we will hear good news about the God who lives and moves among us here and now.

READY TO LISTEN?

Questions to Begin

15 minutes
Use a question or two to get warmed up for the reading.

1   What is your favorite flower? tree? houseplant?

2   Do you enjoy gardening? Why or why not?

Opening the Bible

5 minutes
Read the passage aloud. Let individuals take turns reading paragraphs.

What's Happened

The Gospel of Mark moves at almost breakneck pace. There is little room for reflections or explanations; the Gospel centers simply on Jesus moving from place to place, healing, teaching, and confounding almost everyone who comes in contact with him. The first three chapters of Mark take us immediately to the heart of Jesus' ministry. There is no account of Jesus' birth, as we find in Matthew and Luke. Mark introduces us to Jesus as an adult, in connection with John the Baptist, and then shows Jesus beginning to preach his message of repentance and the coming of God's kingdom.

It is clear from these first three chapters that Jesus is a startling figure to all who encounter him. He heals the ill and infirm. He forgives sins. He and his disciples disregard the Sabbath regulations as interpreted by influential religious leaders called Pharisees. Jesus' healing of a man on the Sabbath in a synagogue (3:1–6), for example, violates the Pharisees' sensibilities about appropriate Sabbath behavior.

Throughout these first three chapters, Mark invites us to consider the knotty question of just who this Jesus might be. Jesus not only speaks *of* God; he seems to speak *for* God. He claims intimacy with God, yet he challenges some people's sense of what being religious means. For these reasons, Mark lets us know, many were puzzled by Jesus' identity. In the last verses of chapter 3, Jesus asserts that there is something about his identity that might even be incomprehensible to his own blood relations, though it will be understood by all—family, friends, or strangers—who do the will of God.

After all this urgent activity, all of these wondrous acts and implicit yet astonishing claims about himself, Jesus settles down in a boat and begins to speak at length. He tells a parable.

The Reading: Mark 4:1–20

A Story about Sowing

¹ Again he began to teach beside the sea. Such a very large crowd gathered around him that he got into a boat on the sea and sat there,

while the whole crowd was beside the sea on the land. 2 He began to teach them many things in parables, and in his teaching he said to them: 3 "Listen! A sower went out to sow. 4 And as he sowed, some seed fell on the path, and the birds came and ate it up. 5 Other seed fell on rocky ground, where it did not have much soil, and it sprang up quickly, since it had no depth of soil. 6 And when the sun rose, it was scorched; and since it had no root, it withered away. 7 Other seed fell among thorns, and the thorns grew up and choked it, and it yielded no grain. 8 Other seed fell into good soil and brought forth grain, growing up and increasing and yielding thirty and sixty and a hundredfold." 9 And he said, "Let anyone with ears to hear listen!"

Why Parables?

10 When he was alone, those who were around him along with the twelve asked him about the parables. 11 And he said to them, "To you has been given the secret of the kingdom of God, but for those outside, everything comes in parables; 12 in order that

'they may indeed look, but not perceive,
    and may indeed listen, but not understand;
so that they may not turn again and be forgiven.'"

Jesus Explains

13 And he said to them, "Do you not understand this parable? Then how will you understand all the parables? 14 The sower sows the word. 15 These are the ones on the path where the word is sown: when they hear, Satan immediately comes and takes away the word that is sown in them. 16 And these are the ones sown on rocky ground: when they hear the word, they immediately receive it with joy. 17 But they have no root, and endure only for a while; then, when trouble or persecution arises on account of the word, immediately they fall away. 18 And others are those sown among the thorns: these are the ones who hear the word, 19 but the cares of the world, and the lure of wealth, and the desire for other things come in and choke the word, and it yields nothing. 20 And these are the ones sown on the good soil: they hear the word and accept it and bear fruit, thirty and sixty and a hundredfold."

10 minutes
Choose questions according to your interest and time.

1 Reread the parable (verses 3–8). Does it mention God or religion? Imagine yourself hearing it for the first time, knowing nothing about Jesus. What do you hear in the parable?

2 To whom does Jesus address his words in verses 3 through 9? in verses 11 through 20? What is the significance of the difference?

3 What does Jesus seem to be saying about the purpose of parables in verses 11 and 12?

4 In his explanation (verses 14 through 20), what does Jesus imply about the role of those in whom the seed is planted? Is it active? passive? both?

A Guide to the Reading

If participants have not read this section already, read it aloud. Otherwise go on to "Questions for Application."

The parable of the sower is found in all three of the synoptic Gospels, and in all three it is the first narrative parable that Jesus tells. The synoptic evangelists obviously saw this parable not only as an excellent introduction to the parables of Jesus but also as the key to understanding all of them (4:13) and, in the process, Jesus as well.

The story Jesus tells in verses 3 to 9 would have been at once familiar and strange to his first listeners. He takes an experience from their everyday life—the risks of sowing—and gives it a twist. The rhythm of the parable leads us to expect some yield at the end, certainly, as the story moves from sowing that is a total loss to sowing that is briefly promising to sowing that grows to a point before dying. The audience would have expected that the final step would be a successful harvest. But they would not have expected what Jesus describes: an almost miraculous harvest, far beyond what any Galilean farmer could have ever hoped to achieve.

After the crowd hears the parable, "those who were around him along with the twelve" (4:10) ask him about it. Notice that Jesus' answer and his explanation of the parable are offered to these people, not to the crowd. The people in the crowd are left to consider the story of the seeds on their own. As they did not seek to know more of the storyteller, it is quite possible that many of them missed the point completely, given the fact that the parable says nothing explicitly about God or faith.

This difficulty in understanding the parable is addressed by Jesus in verses 10 through 12. Yet Jesus' explanation raises more questions than it answers. For in these words, quoted from the prophet Isaiah (Isaiah 6:9–10), Jesus seems to be saying that he tells parables in order to confuse his hearers. He uses parables because they are obstacles to understanding! How can that be?

In part, Jesus may mean that he uses parables because they spur listeners to respond to him. Parables are a puzzling form of teaching, and unless a person is interested enough to follow Jesus and inquire into the meaning of his parables—like the Twelve and "those who were around him"—the parables will remain puzzling. Thus, each of Jesus' parables contains an unstated challenge to the listener: Will you come and follow me in order to understand?

In part, also, Jesus' explanation is probably a way of saying that the failure of many of his listeners to understand him and follow him is somehow within God's plan. On other occasions Jesus speaks about bad things happening "so that the Scripture might be fulfilled" (John 17:12). He does not mean that God has willed evil. Rather, this is a way of saying that God has foreseen people's sin and has taken it into account in his plan. Just as people rejected the prophet Isaiah, Jesus is saying to his disciples, so people will reject him—but God's plan will move on to fulfillment nevertheless. The quotation from Isaiah and the parable, taken together, express Jesus' conviction that while many people will close their ears to his message, their refusal will not derail God's plan, and his ministry will nonetheless have tremendous effect on those who respond to him.

The parable of the sower is unusual among Jesus' parables because he offers an explanation for its meaning. His explanation raises the issue of receptivity. Jesus makes it clear that our receptivity to his word can be limited by many factors: our shallowness, our fear, and our greed. New Testament scholar Morna Hooker writes that after each of the descriptions of the bad soil and frustrated growth, "as with the account of Nathan's parable in 2 Samuel 12, we detect . . . the warning . . . : 'This could mean you!'" The word of God is freely sown, but it is only fruitful in a lasting way when the ground is fertile and receptive.

But Jesus' parable is not just an exhortation to us to examine ourselves. It is, perhaps primarily, a declaration of confidence that God himself is acting. Many people will hear Jesus—and in later centuries, hear about him—without becoming his followers. Others will make some response, but not the sort that brings about a transformation of their lives. Yet, the parable promises, the inherent power of God's word is unlimited in the heart of a person who receives it with faith.

Questions for Application

40 minutes
Choose questions according to your interest and time.

1 Describe times in your life when you have been "rocky" soil. What made you so? Did you change? How?

2 Describe a time in your life when either pressures from other people or distractions of work or money or recreation limited your openness to God. Again, did you change? What have you learned from your experience?

3 What good effects have you experienced when you *have* been open to God's work in your life? How can this experience be an encouragement to you now?

4 How has God sown his seed in your life? Has it come through other people, prayer, books, family, nature, or other means?

5 What practical step can you take to help communicate the gospel to at least one other person?

6 In the view of one commentator, this parable suggests that God sows his word in every corner of the earth. What do you think of that view? What does it mean for evangelization?

Don't be afraid of silences: Some questions take time to answer and some people need time to gather courage to speak.

Stephen Board, *Great Doctrines of the Bible*

Approach to Prayer

15 minutes
Use this approach—or create your own!

◆ Ask someone to read Mark 4:3–9 aloud. Reflect on the reading in silence. Then ask another group member to read the following prayer, pausing for a moment after each line.

Loving God, you sow your seed
in all of our hearts. We
offer you these hearts
today.
Take the hard paths in our
hearts, the places that are
closed to love.
Take the rocky places in our
hearts, the places that are
shallow and faithless.
Take the thorny places in our
hearts, the places that are
choked by selfishness.
Take the fertile places in our
hearts, the places where
your word has taken root.
Take all of these places and
make them your own.
Open what is closed, deepen
what is shallow, water
what is dry, and nurture
what is fertile and rich.
We pray this through your
Word, Jesus our Lord.
Amen.

Saints in the Making

The Seed of the Church

This section is a supplement for individual reading.

Missionaries answer the Christians' call to spread the seeds of faith by traveling to other places to plant those seeds. As Jesus indicates, not all of the seeds will sprout and grow into lasting fruit. Some missionaries never see which seeds will and will not take root. They must serve in faith and hope.

Such was the case with some of the French Jesuit missionaries to Native American communities in Canada in the seventeenth century. The "black robes," as they were called, were welcomed by some of the Native Americans but were objects of suspicion and fear to others. Their presence was blamed for poor crops and epidemics, and they were often used as pawns in the conflicts between warring tribes.

St. Isaac Jogues (1607–46) is one of the better-known of these missionaries. He carried out a mission to the Hurons who lived west of Quebec. In 1642, he journeyed to Montreal to obtain supplies for the sick and hungry people at the mission station. On the way, he was captured by Mohawks, who enslaved him and subjected him to horrific torture. He escaped and returned to Europe with the aid of Dutch tradesmen, but in 1644 he was back in Canada. He even ventured back among the Mohawks as part of a peace mission. On the return trip from this peace mission, some Mohawks captured and killed him, blaming a box of personal belongings he had left behind for an epidemic that had broken out among them. Jogues was martyred in a village called Ossernenon, in what is now northern New York. By all appearances, his time among the Mohawks was fruitless.

But in 1656, a girl was born in Ossernenon to a Mohawk chief and an Algonquin Christian woman. This girl grew up nourished by the small, struggling seedlings of Christianity that had been planted around her by the French missionaries. She was eventually baptized and took the name Catherine—in her language, Kateri. Rejected by her own community for her Christian faith, she moved to a small village of Native American Christians near Montreal, and there she died, after a short but devout life, at the age of twenty-four. In 1980, Kateri Tekakwitha was beatified by the Church. Her faith and virtue were living confirmation of the words of Tertullian in the second century: "The blood of the martyrs is seed"—the seed of the Church.

A Merciful God

Questions to Begin

15 minutes
Use a question or two to get warmed up for the reading.

1 Did you ever get lost as a child? What did it feel like? What did it feel like to be found?

2 What was your first paying job? Did you like it?

Opening the Bible

5 minutes
Read the passage aloud. Let individuals take turns reading
paragraphs.

What's Happened

Jesus often told his parables in response to real questions and
concerns expressed by those around him. The first parable in
this session, from the Gospel of Matthew, is told as a way of
addressing his disciples' concerns about their place in the
kingdom (see Matthew 19:27).

      The second reading relates two parables that use the
experience of losing and finding as a basis for understanding
God's love. These two parables, and the one that follows them
in Luke 15 (on the prodigal son, which is discussed in the Six
Weeks with the Bible book on Luke), are Jesus' answer to the
"grumblings" of the religious leaders who are scandalized by
Jesus' association with notorious sinners.

The Reading: Matthew 20:1–16; Luke 15:1–10

Payday

Matthew 20:1 "For the kingdom of heaven is like a landowner who went
out early in the morning to hire laborers for his vineyard. 2 After
agreeing with the laborers for the usual daily wage, he sent them into
his vineyard. 3 When he went out about nine o'clock, he saw others
standing idle in the marketplace; 4 and he said to them, 'You also go
into the vineyard, and I will pay you whatever is right.' So they went.
5 When he went out again about noon and about three o'clock, he
did the same. 6 And about five o'clock he went out and found others
standing around; and he said to them, 'Why are you standing here idle
all day?' 7 They said to him, 'Because no one has hired us.' He said
to them, 'You also go into the vineyard.' 8 When evening came, the
owner of the vineyard said to his manager, 'Call the laborers and give
them their pay, beginning with the last and then going to the first.'
9 When those hired about five o'clock came, each of them received
the usual daily wage. 10 Now when the first came, they thought
they would receive more; but each of them also received the usual
daily wage. 11 And when they received it, they grumbled against the
landowner, 12 saying, 'These last worked only one hour, and you have

made them equal to us who have borne the burden of the day and the scorching heat.' 13 But he replied to one of them, 'Friend, I am doing you no wrong; did you not agree with me for the usual daily wage? 14 Take what belongs to you and go; I choose to give to this last the same as I give to you. 15 Am I not allowed to do what I choose with what belongs to me? Or are you envious because I am generous?' 16 So the last will be first, and the first will be last."

Lost and Found

Luke 15:1 Now all the tax collectors and sinners were coming near to listen to him. 2 And the Pharisees and the scribes were grumbling and saying, "This fellow welcomes sinners and eats with them."

3 So he told them this parable: 4 "Which one of you, having a hundred sheep and losing one of them, does not leave the ninety-nine in the wilderness and go after the one that is lost until he finds it? 5 When he has found it, he lays it on his shoulders and rejoices. 6 And when he comes home, he calls together his friends and neighbors, saying to them, 'Rejoice with me, for I have found my sheep that was lost.' 7 Just so, I tell you, there will be more joy in heaven over one sinner who repents than over ninety-nine righteous persons who need no repentance.

8 "Or what woman having ten silver coins, if she loses one of them, does not light a lamp, sweep the house, and search carefully until she finds it? 9 When she has found it, she calls together her friends and neighbors, saying, 'Rejoice with me, for I have found the coin that I had lost.' 10 Just so, I tell you, there is joy in the presence of the angels of God over one sinner who repents."

Questions for Careful Reading

10 minutes
Choose questions according to your interest and time.

1 How does the landowner's agreement with the first group of laborers differ from his agreement with the other groups?

2 Why does the first group of workers feel wronged? On what standard do they seem to base their criticism of the landowner's actions?

3 How does the landowner justify his actions? What is his motivation for his treatment of the workers?

4 Is the shepherd's action risky?

5 What do the actions of the shepherd and the woman indicate about their attitude toward what they have lost?

A Guide to the Reading

If participants have not read this section already, read it aloud. Otherwise go on to "Questions for Application."

The images in the parable of the laborers in the vineyard would have been familiar to Jesus' hearers. The vineyard is a frequent image of Israel in the Old Testament (see Isaiah 5:1–7), and it was also common to use an employer or a landowner as a metaphor for God. From the beginning of this parable, then, we know that Jesus is telling us about God's treatment of those working in his kingdom.

The landowner hires a group of laborers in the early morning. He negotiates a wage with this first group, and they go into his vineyard. For reasons that are not explained and, we may assume, are therefore not important, at intervals during the day the landowner goes out and hires more laborers. He does not negotiate a wage with these groups, saying only that he will give them "whatever is right" (verse 4).

The reverse order of payment builds tension. The last group hired is the first group paid; they receive the "usual daily wage"—one denarius. The hearer would have expected that the first group hired, who worked all day as opposed to one hour, would receive more. But they don't. They receive that single denarius, and the owner's generosity toward those who came into the vineyard later angers them.

Jesus is challenging his hearers to think of God's kingdom in a new way. It is not a reward like a wage, recognition commensurate with effort. It's not a bargain between us and God either. While our response to God is certainly crucial in our relationship with him, we do not enter into his kingdom on the basis of our accomplishments. God grants salvation—eternal life—on the basis of his generosity. And his generosity cannot be evaluated according to human standards of justice. It is not our place to stand in judgment of God for his kindness to other people, regardless of how surprising it may be. We are called simply to respond, gratefully and joyfully, whenever God welcomes others, no matter when and no matter how.

In the Gospel of Luke, some Pharisees and scribes are offended by Jesus' association with "sinners"—those who flagrantly reject the standards of justice and morality enshrined in Scripture. When Jesus socializes with these sinners, he is violating the age-old warnings against associating with evildoers (Sirach 12:1–7). But Jesus reveals a new way of thinking about sinners by his socializing, and in these parables as well.

One sheep out of a hundred may not seem to be much of a loss, but its worth might be substantial to a poor shepherd whose income is based on a percentage of the profit from the flock. Nevertheless, the shepherd's single-minded pursuit of his sheep verges on reckless behavior, as he leaves the rest of the flock "in the wilderness," perhaps exposed to danger, to seek the lost.

The owner of the lost coin in the second parable is a woman, the only clear instance in the Gospels when a woman is used as a metaphor for God. Her pursuit of her lost object is as exhaustive, although not as dangerous, as the shepherd's.

Both the shepherd and the woman respond to the finding of the lost in the same way: with joy that must be shared. The shepherd calls together his friends and neighbors, the woman her female friends (the Greek word used for "friends" here is feminine). Luke follows these two parables with the parable of the prodigal son, which also ends with a celebration for the one who has been lost and is now found.

The Pharisees and Jesus agree that some are lost. The difference lies in their response to this fact. The Pharisees shun the lost, perhaps as a way of demonstrating that the community rejects their transgressing God's law. The Pharisees do not deny the possibility of forgiveness for sinners, but they believe that it must be earned through sacrifice in the Jerusalem temple and restitution. They are appalled that Jesus is calling sinners to God *through a relationship with himself* rather than through the traditional means.

Jesus, by contrast, reflects the approach of a God who does not let such considerations stand in the way of reconciliation. It is not that Jesus is opposed in principle to community norms of behavior or temple sacrifices (Matthew 18:17; Mark 1:44). But God's single-minded love for the lost trumps these other concerns. Jesus' parables reveal that although we are lost, God is always seeking us. Our conversion comes simply by responding to this God who seeks us in love and rejoices when we are found.

Questions for Application

40 minutes
Choose questions according to your interest and time.

---

1 Are there people you know or know of who have come to God relatively late in their lives? Have you felt resentful of them? What does the parable have to say on this subject?

---

2 What are the differences between trying to earn God's love and living in response to his love? Have you felt that you must do things to earn God's love?

---

3 Have you ever been among the lost? How did it happen? What did you do about it?

---

4 What circumstances in your life has God used to "find" you? How often can this happen in a person's life?

5 Jesus makes it clear that God rejoices when a person willingly responds to his generous love. How could an awareness of this affect your prayer to God? your relationships with the people who are closest to you?

6 Is there sometimes a difference in the way we hope God will treat our sins and the way we think God should treat the sins of others? Discuss this attitude—and what light these parables shed on it.

Encourage one another to participate. People remember best what they discover and verbalize for themselves.

Winnie Christensen, *Women Who Achieved for God*

Approach to Prayer

15 minutes
Use this approach—or create your own!

◆ Invite the members of the group to take a few moments to silently thank God for showing mercy in their lives. Then ask one member to read Psalm 103:1–13 aloud slowly, pausing between each verse, letting participants voice brief prayers if they like.

A Living Tradition

When the Lost Are Found

This section is a supplement for individual reading.

As bishop of the African city of Carthage, St. Cyprian (d.-258) dealt with many problems. One of the most persistent was the question of what to do with Christians who had publicly denied their faith in the face of persecution but later sought to return to the Church. Some Christians believed that such people should be prohibited from returning. In a letter to a fellow bishop, Cyprian explains why this approach is counter to the gospel.

While the Lord left the ninety-nine that were safe, and sought after the one wandering and weary, taking it on his shoulders and carrying it when he'd found it, we not only do not seek the fallen but even drive them away when they come to us: and while false prophets are still tearing apart Christ's flock, we open the flock to dogs and wolves, so that those who survive persecution are ruined by our own hardness and inhumanity.

Considering God's love and mercy, we should not be so bitter and cruel, but we should mourn with those who mourn, weep with those who weep and raise them up as much as we can by the help and comfort of our love; neither being harsh and stubborn in rejecting their repentance, nor being too lax in bringing them back into communion too quickly. Look! A wounded brother lies stricken by the enemy in the field of battle. The devil is trying to kill him, but Christ is calling us to show mercy so that those He has redeemed may not be lost. Which of these two do we assist? On whose side do we stand?

How to Pray

Questions to Begin

15 minutes
Use a question or two to get warmed up for the reading.

1 What kind of sleeper are you?
❑ I sleep soundly.
❑ My nights are restless.
❑ Sleep? What's that?

2 Have you ever watched a court in session, either in person or on television? If so, what was your impression of the judge?

3 In your church, do people tend to sit in the same spot every week, or do they change their seats from week to week? Where do you sit in church? Why?

5 minutes
Read the passage aloud. Let individuals take turns reading
paragraphs.

What's Happened

Jesus tells the first parable here (from Luke 11) in the context
of answering questions about praying. He presents the parable
immediately after teaching his disciples the Lord's Prayer. The
second and third parables this week (from Luke 18) follow Jesus'
teaching about how to relate to God as we wait for the final coming
of God's kingdom (Luke 17:20–37).

The Reading: Luke 11:5–10; 18:1–14

Are You Sleeping?

5 And he said to them, "Suppose one of you has a friend, and you go
to him at midnight and say to him, 'Friend, lend me three loaves of
bread; 6 for a friend of mine has arrived, and I have nothing to set
before him.' 7 And he answers from within, 'Do not bother me; the
door has already been locked, and my children are with me in bed;
I cannot get up and give you anything.' 8 I tell you, even though he
will not get up and give him anything because he is his friend, at
least because of his persistence he will get up and give him whatever
he needs.

9 "So I say to you, Ask, and it will be given you; search, and
you will find; knock, and the door will be opened for you. 10 For
everyone who asks receives, and everyone who searches finds, and
for everyone who knocks, the door will be opened."

A Fearless Woman

18:1 Then Jesus told them a parable about their need to pray always
and not to lose heart. 2 He said, "In a certain city there was a judge
who neither feared God nor had respect for people. 3 In that city
there was a widow who kept coming to him and saying, 'Grant me
justice against my opponent.' 4 For a while he refused; but later he
said to himself, 'Though I have no fear of God and no respect for
anyone, 5 yet because this widow keeps bothering me, I will grant
her justice, so that she may not wear me out by continually coming.'"
6 And the Lord said, "Listen to what the unjust judge says. 7 And

will not God grant justice to his chosen ones who cry to him day and night? Will he delay long in helping them? [8] I tell you, he will quickly grant justice to them. And yet, when the Son of Man comes, will he find faith on earth?"

Standing before God

[9] He also told this parable to some who trusted in themselves that they were righteous and regarded others with contempt: [10] "Two men went up to the temple to pray, one a Pharisee and the other a tax collector. [11] The Pharisee, standing by himself, was praying thus, 'God, I thank you that I am not like other people: thieves, rogues, adulterers, or even like this tax collector. [12] I fast twice a week; I give a tenth of all my income.' [13] But the tax collector, standing far off, would not even look up to heaven, but was beating his breast and saying, 'God, be merciful to me, a sinner!' [14] I tell you, this man went down to his home justified rather than the other; for all who exalt themselves will be humbled, but all who humble themselves will be exalted."

10 minutes
Choose questions according to your interest and time.

1 In the first parable, why is the neighbor reluctant to rise? What finally convinces him?

2 What is surprising about the parable of the judge and the widow?

3 In the first two parables, Jesus uses human beings with faulty motives as metaphors for God. Why?

4 Is the Pharisee an arrogant man? Why or why not?

5 What is the difference between the Pharisee's attitude toward God and the tax collector's?

A Guide to the Reading

If participants have not read this section already, read it aloud. Otherwise go on to "Questions for Application."

In the parable of the homeowner with an unexpected guest, Jesus builds a story rooted in his listeners' understanding of hospitality. In the culture of the time, hospitality was an almost sacred obligation. The situation that Jesus describes—a visitor arriving in the middle of the night, the host caught short, a neighbor awakened to help meet the obligation—may have been unusual to his listeners, but the end result would not have seemed surprising to them. They would have done the same if they had found themselves in the sandals of either of the men in the story. Like the neighbor awakened by the midnight request, they might have grumbled, because meeting the host's needs would have entailed waking up the family members, who would have all been sleeping together in the single-room house. But they would have done what he did and provided the loaves, because the honor of the village would have required it.

Jesus indicates that in the end the neighbor responds not only out of a sense of duty and a fear of shaming his entire community, but also because of the host's troublesome "persistence" (Luke 11:8). If a human being responds to such a good request, Jesus is saying, even if it is offered in a manner that violates ordinary standards of politeness (that annoying "persistence"), won't God be even more likely to answer people's prayers?

Jesus' listeners would have had preconceived impressions of the two characters in the second parable: widows were dependent on others and therefore merited special respect, and judges were charged with rendering fair judgment, based on fear of the Lord (2 Chronicles 19:5–7). But, as is often the case with Jesus' parables, the characters go against these preconceptions. This judge lacks any regard for what is right. And this widow, while she is socially dependent, is anything but weak. She comes to the judge directly, without a male intercessor and without resorting to bribery (common in those times), and addresses him without any groveling. She simply demands what is her due.

There is no sentimental ending here. The judge is not converted. He does not agree to the widow's demands out of any honorable motive. He just wants her to stop bothering him. The word that is here translated as "wear me out" (Luke 18:5) also means "give me a black eye." There's a bit of humor in the image of the supposedly weak widow making the powerful judge see things her way. Once again, a petitioner shatters expectations by defying standards of making a request.

In these parables Jesus is not suggesting that God must be roused from sleep to respond to our prayers or browbeaten into answering them. He is saying, rather, that we should approach God without regard to what the world says is proper and reasonable. Some religious people might say that prayer must be offered in a certain form. Jesus tells us to ignore such concerns and simply approach God directly with our needs—and with persistence!

The final parable, of the Pharisee and the tax collector, takes us into the heart of the one who prays. To the first hearers of this parable, the Pharisee would not have seemed to be an arrogant man. The prayer that he utters is similar to common Jewish prayers of the time. The Pharisee is, in fact, an eminently religious person. Jesus' listeners would not have given him a negative evaluation.

What would have surprised them is the presence of a tax collector in the temple. Tax collecting customarily involved extortion, which would be understood as sinful behavior. Even more shocking is that the tax collector does not evidently seek to repent. He makes no restitution for what he has unjustly collected—as another tax collector, named Zacchaeus, does in the next chapter (Luke 19:1–10). This tax collector asks God for mercy, then leaves without renouncing his line of work, yet Jesus pronounces him righteous! And not the Pharisee!

The key difference between the two men is that the tax collector recognizes his sinfulness while the Pharisee is quite aware of the sinfulness of others but blind to his own. Jesus' listeners might well have prayed like the Pharisee and may have been equally blind to their own failings. By their initial identification with the Pharisee, they would have been trapped by Jesus into seeing, in the end, what the Pharisee did not: that they were more like the tax collector than outward appearance indicated.

When we embrace the same awareness, Jesus' parable implies, we can really begin to pray.

Questions for Application

40 minutes
Choose questions according to your interest and time.

1   Have you ever prayed for
something for a long time and
felt that your prayer was fruitless
or not worthy of God's attention?
What do these parables say
about that feeling?

2   In these first two parables,
Jesus calls for boldness and
directness in prayer. How does
your own approach to God
in prayer compare with the
approach that Jesus evokes
in these parables? What could
you learn from them?

3   What kinds of considerations
hold you back from being totally
honest with God in your prayer?
How can you overcome these
obstacles?

4 In his prayer, the Pharisee compares himself favorably to others. Are there people with whom you are tempted to compare yourself?

5 Taken together, these parables suggest that in prayer we should approach God boldly, honestly, and with great humility. Are these contradictory attitudes? How can we be bold, honest, and humble with God at the same time in our prayer?

Pray for each member of the Bible study group by name often through the week.

Ed Stewart and Nina Fishwick, *Grouptalk*

Approach to Prayer

15 minutes
Use this approach—or create your own!

◆ Invite members of the group to share, as boldly as the widow coming before the judge, any needs they would like to bring to the Lord during this prayer time. Then ask one member of the group to pray the Our Father aloud slowly, pausing for a moment of reflection after each line. Finally, pray the Our Father aloud together as a group.

Saints in the Making

The Power of Prayer

This section is a supplement for individual reading.

St. Thérèse of Lisieux (1873–97) lived a short twenty-four years, but the impact of her life and spirituality has been enormous. In this passage from *Story of a Soul,* her autobiography, Thérèse writes of her faith in the power of prayer, as well as her difficulties with it.

How great is the power of Prayer! One could call it a Queen who has at each instant free access to the King and who is able to obtain whatever she asks. To be heard it is not necessary to read from a book some beautiful formula composed for the occasion. If this were the case, alas, I would have to be pitied! Outside the Divine Office, which I am very unworthy to recite, I do not have the courage to force myself to search out beautiful prayers in books. There are so many of them it really gives me a headache! and each prayer is more beautiful than the others. I cannot recite them all, and not knowing which to choose, I do like children who do not know how to read, I say very simply to God what I wish to say, without composing beautiful sentences, and He always understands me. For me, prayer is an aspiration of the heart, it is a simple glance directed to heaven, it is a cry of gratitude and love in the midst of trial as well as joy; finally, it is something great, supernatural, which expands my soul and unites me to Jesus!

I force myself in vain to meditate on the mysteries of the rosary; I don't succeed in fixing my mind on them. For a long time I was desolate about this lack of devotion which astonished me, for I love the Blessed Virgin so much that it should be easy for me to recite in her honor prayers which are so pleasing to her. Now I am less desolate. . . . Sometimes when my mind is in such aridity that it is impossible to draw forth one single thought to unite me with God, I very slowly recite an "Our Father" and then the angelic salutation [the Hail Mary]; then these prayers give me great delight; they nourish my soul much more than if I had recited them precipitately a hundred times.

WHICH OF THESE?

Questions to Begin

15 minutes
Use a question or two to get warmed up for the reading.

---

1 We make all kinds of promises to ourselves and to others. What kinds of promises are difficult to keep?

---

2 If your neighbors were asked to describe you, what do you think they'd say?

Opening the Bible

5 minutes
Read the passage aloud. Let individuals take turns reading
paragraphs.

What's Happened

The first parable in this week's reading is directed at priests and
scribes who have gathered in the temple area and are questioning
the source of Jesus' authority. Jesus tells this parable to shed light
on how they are responding both to his ministry and to that of John
the Baptist.

We find the second parable, known as the parable of the
Good Samaritan, in a chapter of Luke's Gospel that is centered
on discipleship (Luke 10). The parable is told as an answer to the
question of a scholar of the Scriptures who has become aware of
Jesus' startling words and deeds. The scholar asks the question
although he should be confident that he already knows the answer—
perhaps his conversation with Jesus indicates that he is beginning
to wonder if his own answers are indeed correct.

The Reading: Matthew 21:28–32; Luke 10:25–37

A Promise Broken

Matthew 21:28 "What do you think? A man had two sons; he went to
the first and said, 'Son, go and work in the vineyard today.' 29 He
answered, 'I will not'; but later he changed his mind and went. 30 The
father went to the second and said the same; and he answered, 'I go,
sir'; but he did not go. 31 Which of the two did the will of his father?"
They said, "The first." Jesus said to them, "Truly I tell you, the tax
collectors and the prostitutes are going into the kingdom of God
ahead of you. 32 For John came to you in the way of righteousness
and you did not believe him, but the tax collectors and the prostitutes
believed him; and even after you saw it, you did not change your
minds and believe him."

On the Road

Luke 10:25 Just then a lawyer stood up to test Jesus. "Teacher," he said,
"what must I do to inherit eternal life?" 26 He said to him, "What is
written in the law? What do you read there?" 27 He answered, "You

shall love the Lord your God with all your heart, and with all your soul, and with all your strength, and with all your mind; and your neighbor as yourself." 28 And he said to him, "You have given the right answer; do this, and you will live."

29 But wanting to justify himself, he asked Jesus, "And who is my neighbor?" 30 Jesus replied, "A man was going down from Jerusalem to Jericho, and fell into the hands of robbers, who stripped him, beat him, and went away, leaving him half dead. 31 Now by chance a priest was going down that road; and when he saw him, he passed by on the other side. 32 So likewise a Levite, when he came to the place and saw him, passed by on the other side. 33 But a Samaritan while traveling came near him; and when he saw him, he was moved with pity. 34 He went to him and bandaged his wounds, having poured oil and wine on them. Then he put him on his own animal, brought him to an inn, and took care of him. 35 The next day he took out two denarii, gave them to the innkeeper, and said, 'Take care of him; and when I come back, I will repay you whatever more you spend.' 36 Which of these three, do you think, was a neighbor to the man who fell into the hands of the robbers?" 37 He said, "The one who showed him mercy." Jesus said to him, "Go and do likewise."

Questions for Careful Reading

10 minutes
Choose questions according to your interest and time.

1 In the first story, how do Jesus' listeners condemn themselves in their answer to his question in verse 31?

2 Luke says that the lawyer in the second parable was trying to "justify himself" in his final question to Jesus. What does this seem to mean?

3 The robbery victim was stripped of all his clothing and was left unconscious. How might this have affected the first two travelers' decisions not to assist him?

4 All three passersby "see" the wounded man. What happens to the Samaritan after that initial seeing that seems to escape the other two?

5 The lawyer originally wanted to know who his neighbor was. Does Jesus' parable answer his question?

A Guide to the Reading

If participants have not read this section already, read it aloud. Otherwise go on to "Questions for Application."

This first parable is, on the surface, about family, but a close listening reveals that it is really about who is genuinely religious—who is truly doing God's will. The first son's initial refusal to work is a rebellious act. The second son seems to be the opposite of his brother. Anything but rebellious, he speaks deferentially to his father, calling him "sir" (Matthew 21:30; the Greek word may even be translated as "lord").

But in the end, it is the rebellious son who does the father's will and the supposedly obedient son who ignores it. The question Jesus poses in verse 31 would have forced his first listeners to recognize their own failures. For John the Baptist was an authentic prophet and they refused to repent in response to his preaching, and thus they were the second son, while the sinners who came to John and repented ended up doing the will of the Father. The parable points up the fact that a relationship with God requires more than speaking the right words.

The next parable also deals with the possible gap between maintaining the outward forms of religious observance and carrying out God's will. A lawyer and Jesus are discussing the command "You shall love your neighbor as yourself." The lawyer asks Jesus to define *neighbor* so that he can know whom this command requires him to care for. The lawyer is thinking that there are insiders whom he is required to help and outsiders to whom he has no moral obligation. Perhaps he has recalled passages such as Sirach 12:1–7, which warns against strengthening evildoers by giving them any kind of assistance. The lawyer wants to make sure he has his bases covered and that everyone on God's list is on his list as well.

The road from Jerusalem to Jericho was, as the first-century Jewish historian Josephus described it, "desolate and rocky." It was also a road that literally went "down" (Luke 10:30). Jerusalem is at an elevation of 2,500 feet above sea level; Jericho is 820 feet below—a drop of 3,300 feet in seventeen miles.

We are never given any identifying information about the victim of the crime. He is stripped and left "half dead," that is, unconscious. Thus he cannot be identified by either dress or speech. We do not know who he is, and neither do his potential rescuers.

The first to pass by is a priest, possibly on his way home from his two-week stint offering sacrifice at the Jerusalem temple. Why does he not stop? We are not given a reason, but a few would have occurred to Jesus' listeners. First, there was the question of identity. If the man was a sinner, the priest would have felt disinclined to help him. Second, if the man was dead, the priest would have made himself ritually impure just by touching the corpse—and besides, he was forbidden by the law to come within a dozen feet of the corpse. Third, he might have feared being assailed by robbers if he stopped to help the man.

Similar concerns would have been in the Levite's mind. If he was on his way *to* Jerusalem (Jesus does not say which direction he was going), he would have wanted to avoid any possible ritual impurity from touching the corpse because purification would require a seven-day period of cleansing, during which time he would not be able to work in the temple.

Help finally arrives in the person of the Samaritan. Samaritans saw themselves as children of Israel but were considered apostates by the Jews. The language that Jesus uses to describe the Samaritan's actions evokes Old Testament descriptions of God's care for his people. The Samaritan had *pity*—a word often used to refer to God's attitude toward the suffering. He binds the man's wounds as God is described as doing in Hosea 6:1.

The Samaritan takes a risk by bringing the man to an inn in a Jewish area. As a Samaritan, he is likely to meet with hostility. He gives the innkeeper enough money to care for the man for a week or two. Otherwise, the man would have been indebted to the innkeeper.

In the end, the lawyer's question has been turned on him. There are no lists, no insiders or outsiders. The question is no longer "Who is my neighbor?" but "To whom must I be a neighbor?"

Both parables reveal the need to beware self-deception. Our religious observances are important, but we cannot let our religious speech lull us into complacency about our relationship with God, just as we cannot let our religious activities become a barrier between us and the people who need our help.

Questions for Application

40 minutes
Choose questions according to your interest and time.

1 What factors might influence us to say no to the Lord and later change our mind?

2 What factors sometimes influence us to say yes to the Lord and later change our mind?

3 The priest and the Levite consider other concerns to be more vital than helping another human being in need. Are there concerns that you, by your actions, consider more important than helping needy neighbors? (Who are your needy neighbors?)

4 What risks do you take in reaching out to others in love and compassion?

5 What is the message of this parable for you? Whom do you have the most difficult time seeing as a neighbor? How might this parable help you overcome this difficulty?

Don't be content with just one answer. Ask, "What do the rest of you think?" or "Anything else?" until several people have given answers to the question.

Andrea Sterk and Peter Scazzero, *Christian Character*

Approach to Prayer

15 minutes
Use this approach—or create your own!

♦ Allow the group to take a few moments to pray quietly, perhaps focusing on gratitude for the opportunities God provides to serve him and his people. Then pray aloud together the following prayer by Cardinal John Henry Newman, adapted by Mother Teresa of Calcutta:

Dear Jesus, help us to spread
Your fragrance everywhere
we go.
Flood our souls with Your spirit
and life.
Penetrate and possess our whole
being so utterly that
our lives may only be a
radiance of Yours.
Shine through us, and be so in us
that every soul we come in
contact with may feel Your
presence in our soul.
Let them look up and see no
longer us, but only Jesus.

A Living Tradition

Promising without Doing

This section is a supplement for individual reading.

Cardinal John Henry Newman (1801–90) was a convert to Roman Catholicism from Anglicanism. The following reflection on the parable of the two sons is taken from a sermon he preached in an Anglican parish before he entered the Catholic Church.

[What we say we believe is more distant from how we act], than we ourselves are aware. We know generally that it is our duty to serve God, and we resolve we will do so faithfully. We are sincere in thus generally desiring and purposing to be obedient, and we think we are in earnest; yet we go away, and presently, without any struggle of mind or apparent change of purpose, almost without knowing ourselves what we do—we go away and do the very contrary to the resolution we have expressed. . . .

You will observe that in the case of the first son, who said he would not go work and yet did go, it is said, "afterward he repented." He underwent a positive change of purpose. But in the case of the second, it is merely said; "He answered, I go, Sir; and went not," for here there was *no* revolution of sentiment, nothing deliberate; he merely acted according to his habitual frame of mind. He did *not* go work because it was contrary to his general character to work; only he did not know this. He said, "I go, Sir," sincerely, from the feeling of the moment; but when the words were out of his mouth, then they were forgotten. It was like the wind blowing against a stream, which seems for a moment to change its course in consequence, but in fact flows down as before. . . .

He who does one little deed of obedience, whether he denies himself some comfort to relieve the sick and needy, or curbs his temper, or forgives an enemy, or asks forgiveness for an offence committed by him, or resists the clamor or ridicule of the world—such a one (as far as we are given to judge) evinces more true faith than could be shown by the most fluent religious conversation, the most intimate knowledge of Scripture doctrine, or the most remarkable agitation and change of religious sentiments.

GOD CALLS

Questions to Begin

15 minutes
Use a question or two to get warmed up for the reading.

1 What would you do if you won the lottery?

2 What do you do when you are invited to an event you really don't want to attend?
❏ I grin and bear it.
❏ I go, but I make sure that I don't enjoy myself.
❏ I decline graciously without an explanation.
❏ I suddenly discover long-lost sick relatives.

5

Opening the Bible

5 minutes
*Read the passage aloud. Let individuals take turns reading
paragraphs.*

What's Happened

The first parable in this week's reading (from Matthew 25) is part
of Jesus' final teaching session with his disciples in the Gospel of
Matthew. They are in Jerusalem in the days preceding his arrest, and
Jesus has made it clear to his disciples that he will be leaving them.
Difficult times are on the horizon, but he will return. The parable
deals with what it means for his followers to live in response to his
call while awaiting his return.

The second parable we will read this week (from Luke 14) is
about a banquet, which Jesus tells while dining at a banquet.

The Reading: Matthew 25:14–30; Luke 14:15–24

Playing It Safe

Matthew 25:14 "For it is as if a man, going on a journey, summoned
his slaves and entrusted his property to them; 15 to one he gave five
talents, to another two, to another one, to each according to his
ability. Then he went away. 16 The one who had received the five
talents went off at once and traded with them, and made five more
talents. 17 In the same way, the one who had the two talents made
two more talents. 18 But the one who had received the one talent
went off and dug a hole in the ground and hid his master's money.
19 After a long time the master of those slaves came and settled
accounts with them. 20 Then the one who had received the five
talents came forward, bringing five more talents, saying, 'Master,
you handed over to me five talents; see, I have made five more
talents.' 21 His master said to him, 'Well done, good and trustworthy
slave; you have been trustworthy in a few things, I will put you in
charge of many things; enter into the joy of your master.' 22 And the
one with the two talents also came forward, saying, 'Master, you
handed over to me two talents; see, I have made two more talents.'
23 His master said to him, 'Well done, good and trustworthy slave;
you have been trustworthy in a few things, I will put you in charge
of many things; enter into the joy of your master.' 24 Then the one
who had received the one talent also came forward, saying, 'Master,

I knew that you were a harsh man, reaping where you did not sow, and gathering where you did not scatter seed; 25 so I was afraid, and I went and hid your talent in the ground. Here you have what is yours.' 26 But his master replied, 'You wicked and lazy slave! You knew, did you, that I reap where I did not sow, and gather where I did not scatter? 27 Then you ought to have invested my money with the bankers, and on my return I would have received what was my own with interest. 28 So take the talent from him, and give it to the one with the ten talents. 29 For to all those who have, more will be given, and they will have an abundance; but from those who have nothing, even what they have will be taken away. 30 As for this worthless slave, throw him into the outer darkness, where there will be weeping and gnashing of teeth.'"

Regrets Only

Luke 14:15 One of the dinner guests, on hearing this, said to him, "Blessed is anyone who will eat bread in the kingdom of God!" 16 Then Jesus said to him, "Someone gave a great dinner and invited many. 17 At the time for the dinner he sent his slave to say to those who had been invited, 'Come; for everything is ready now.' 18 But they all alike began to make excuses. The first said to him, 'I have bought a piece of land, and I must go out and see it; please accept my regrets.' 19 Another said, 'I have bought five yoke of oxen, and I am going to try them out; please accept my regrets.' 20 Another said, 'I have just been married, and therefore I cannot come.' 21 So the slave returned and reported this to his master. Then the owner of the house became angry and said to his slave, 'Go out at once into the streets and lanes of the town and bring in the poor, the crippled, the blind, and the lame.' 22 And the slave said, 'Sir, what you ordered has been done, and there is still room.' 23 Then the master said to the slave, 'Go out into the roads and lanes, and compel people to come in, so that my house may be filled. 24 For I tell you, none of those who were invited will taste my dinner.'"

Questions for Careful Reading

10 minutes
Choose questions according to your interest and time.

1 What does the master's reaction to his servants' actions indicate about what he values?

2 How does the third servant explain his behavior? How is this explanation different from his master's analysis?

3 What other choices could each of the invited guests have made instead of sending their regrets to the dinner host? What do their choices reveal about their priorities?

4 What does the size of the banquet in this parable imply about the size of God's kingdom?

5 In what sense is this parable hopeful? In what sense is it a warning?

A Guide to the Reading

If participants have not read this section already, read it aloud. Otherwise go on to "Questions for Application."

Jesus tells the parable of the talents to help his disciples understand their challenges and responsibilities in the days to come. Jesus will be leaving, but he will return. How are his disciples to live in the meantime?

The word *talent* in this parable does not refer to personal abilities. Here it means a measure of weight, specifically of silver. As a measure of precious metal, a talent represents a monetary value. One talent was worth six thousand denarii. A denarius was the ancient minimum daily wage, so a talent was the amount of money an ordinary laborer could earn in twenty years. The master is entrusting his slaves with a major responsibility.

The first two servants get busy and "trade" with their talents—in other words, they do business. The third, out of fear of losing the money and being punished, buries his single talent—a common way to keep treasure safe in the ancient world. When the master returns, he praises the first two servants but turns on the third in fury. Why? The first two servants took risks. The third played it safe. The first two were bold. The third was governed by fear—and, according to the master, by laziness. Jesus is letting us know that we are to act boldly to take advantage of opportunities to advance God's kingdom.

Every Christian has a choice: to work with what the Lord gives us and enter into his joy or to wait in fear and be a spectator to the joy of others. We may wonder what harm there is in spending our lives cautiously. Jesus' final words in this parable make it clear that we do, indeed, have something to lose.

As the second parable begins, dinner guests are called to gather for a banquet. The banquet is a common image for the kingdom of God and for the joy of God's final triumph over evil. The most powerful expression of this in the Old Testament may be Isaiah 25:6–9, in which God invites the entire world to a great mountaintop banquet.

In the Near East in Jesus' time, and still today in rural communities, two invitations were issued to a banquet. The first went out well in advance to determine the number who would attend and the amount of food that would be required. The second went out when the meal was ready. This is the call in the parable.

It was obviously a serious matter, even an insult, if those who accepted the first invitation declined the second. The excuses of those who decline might have indeed been perceived by Jesus' listeners as offensive. The guests who have purchased a field and a team of oxen have surely examined their acquisitions already, since they certainly would not have made their purchases sight unseen. The groom did not get married without advance planning. He must have known of his impending wedding when he accepted the first invitation. In short, those who decline this second call to the banquet are insulting the host by lying and putting their own concerns before their relationship with him.

So the host issues another call. He tells his servant to go and gather the sick and infirm in the town—the list is reminiscent of Jesus' list of those he has come to save (Luke 7:22). This second guest list is a rebuke to the first invitees. The poor have no fields to check or oxen to test; the very poor cannot even afford to celebrate a marriage with a large wedding feast. By implication, the second guest list is also a corrective to those within Judaism who would exclude the imperfect from God's kingdom and to those who deem the concerns of this world more important than a relationship with God.

The master then sends his servant even farther, to gather those outside the community. They are to be compelled to come (Luke 14:23)—not forced, but convinced. They will need persuading because they would react to a generous invitation from a stranger with surprise and even suspicion.

Through his parable, Jesus is suggesting that God has sent out the first invitation to his banquet through his prophets. The second invitation is now offered through himself, and the invitation welcomes all people to a feast at which there is always plenty of room.

Will we work enthusiastically with what God has given us? Will we accept his invitation to the feast, or do we have other things to do? He will be evaluating our responses sooner than we think.

Questions for Application

40 minutes
Choose questions according to your interest and time.

1 In the first parable, the first two servants take risks that result in rewards. When have you taken a risk that bore surprising fruit?

2 In what ways are you afraid of following Jesus with your whole life? What are you afraid you might lose? What do these parables suggest you do about this fear?

3 What does the image of a banquet suggest about the nature of life with God?

---

4 If you were to retell the second parable in a modern setting, what excuses would your first group of invitees give for not being able to attend the banquet?

---

5 What does your church community do to extend the invitation of God's welcoming love to those outside it? How can you help build on this beginning?

---

6 Why is it sometimes difficult to believe that all people really are loved by God? What can be done to overcome this difficulty?

Try to be affirming whenever possible. Never reject an answer.

Eugene Peterson, *Psalms: Prayers of the Heart*

Approach to Prayer

15 minutes
Use this approach—or create your own!

◆ Ask group members to take a few moments to think about what their priorities in life are right now. Invite members to present these priorities honestly to the Lord in silent prayer. After a few moments, pray the following together:

Lord, we come to you in
    gratitude.
We thank you for the gift of our
    lives.
We ask forgiveness for those
    times
In which we have used that gift
    unwisely.
We pray for the courage to open
    ourselves
To your gift of life more fully,
To put you first in all our
    choices,
And to answer yes to your
    invitation to love
Whenever it may come.

A Living Tradition

The Power of Prayer

This section is a supplement for individual reading.

Since early in the history of the Church, Christians have gathered in communities of prayer and work. St. Benedict of Nursia (c. 480–c. 550), the "father of Western monasticism," formulated a pattern of life, or Rule, for communities of monks that is still followed to some degree by most Western monasteries today.

In this passage from his Rule, Benedict calls monks to adopt the welcoming love of God that is reflected in the parable of the banquet.

All who arrive as guests are to be welcomed like Christ, for he is going to say, "I was a stranger and you welcomed me" [Matthew 25:35]. The respect due to their station is to be shown to all, particularly to those of one family with us in the faith [Galatians 6:10] and to pilgrims. As soon as a guest is announced he should be met by the superior or by brethren with every expression of charity. . . . When guests arrive or depart the greatest humility should be shown in addressing them: so, let Christ who is received in them be adored with bowed head or prostrate body.

So when the guests have been welcomed, they should be led to prayer, and then either the superior or someone delegated by him should sit with them. The Divine Law should be read to them for their edification, and after this every kindness should be shown to them. The superior may break the fast for the sake of a guest unless it happens to be an important fast day which cannot be waived. . . . The Abbot should give all the guests water to wash their hands, and with the whole community he should wash their feet. When they have done so, they should recite the verse, "We have received your mercy, O God, in the midst of your temple" [Psalm 48:9]. Special care is to be shown in the reception of the poor and of pilgrims, for in them especially is Christ received; for the awe felt for the wealthy imposes respect enough of itself.

AWAKE FOR THE LORD

Questions to Begin

15 minutes
Use a question or two to get warmed up for the reading.

---

1   What do you do to pass the time when you are required to wait in line or for an appointment?

---

2   What do you do to keep yourself awake and alert when you're tired?

---

3   Are you generally an organized or an unorganized person? Are you happy with this aspect of your personality?

Opening the Bible

5 minutes
Read the passage aloud. Let individuals take turns reading
paragraphs.

What's Happened

In Luke 12, Jesus presents his followers with a portrait of
discipleship. He speaks of courage under persecution (Luke 12:4–9),
the foolishness of hoarding wealth (Luke 12:16–21), dependence
on God (Luke 12:22–34), and in two of the parables we will read
this week, what they, as his servants, should be mindful of when
he departs.

    The third parable in this week's reading is found near the
end of the Gospel of Matthew, when Jesus has arrived in Jerusalem
with his disciples. He tells a series of parables about waiting,
absence, and final judgment, including this one.

The Reading: Luke 12:35–48; Matthew 25:1–13

Ready and Waiting

Luke 12:35 "Be dressed for action and have your lamps lit; 36 be like
those who are waiting for their master to return from the wedding
banquet, so that they may open the door for him as soon as he comes
and knocks. 37 Blessed are those slaves whom the master finds alert
when he comes; truly I tell you, he will fasten his belt and have them
sit down to eat, and he will come and serve them. 38 If he comes
during the middle of the night, or near dawn, and finds them so,
blessed are those slaves.

    39 "But know this: if the owner of the house had known at
what hour the thief was coming, he would not have let his house be
broken into. 40 You also must be ready, for the Son of Man is coming
at an unexpected hour."

Taking Advantage

41 Peter said, "Lord, are you telling this parable for us or for
everyone?" 42 And the Lord said, "Who then is the faithful and
prudent manager whom his master will put in charge of his
slaves, to give them their allowance of food at the proper time?
43 Blessed is that slave whom his master will find at work when

he arrives. 44 Truly I tell you, he will put that one in charge of all his possessions. 45 But if that slave says to himself, 'My master is delayed in coming,' and if he begins to beat the other slaves, men and women, and to eat and drink and get drunk, 46 the master of that slave will come on a day when he does not expect him and at an hour that he does not know, and will cut him in pieces, and put him with the unfaithful. 47 That slave who knew what his master wanted, but did not prepare himself or do what was wanted, will receive a severe beating. 48 But the one who did not know and did what deserved a beating will receive a light beating. From everyone to whom much has been given, much will be required; and from the one to whom much has been entrusted, even more will be demanded."

Too Little Too Late

Matthew 25:1 "Then the kingdom of heaven will be like this. Ten bridesmaids took their lamps and went to meet the bridegroom. 2 Five of them were foolish, and five were wise. 3 When the foolish took their lamps, they took no oil with them; 4 but the wise took flasks of oil with their lamps. 5 As the bridegroom was delayed, all of them became drowsy and slept. 6 But at midnight there was a shout, 'Look! Here is the bridegroom! Come out to meet him.' 7 Then all those bridesmaids got up and trimmed their lamps. 8 The foolish said to the wise, 'Give us some of your oil, for our lamps are going out.' 9 But the wise replied, 'No! there will not be enough for you and for us; you had better go to the dealers and buy some for yourselves.' 10 And while they went to buy it, the bridegroom came, and those who were ready went with him into the wedding banquet; and the door was shut. 11 Later the other bridesmaids came also, saying, 'Lord, lord, open to us.' 12 But he replied, 'Truly I tell you, I do not know you.' 13 Keep awake therefore, for you know neither the day nor the hour."

10 minutes
Choose questions according to your interest and time.

1 What is surprising about the master's actions in the first parable?

2 In the second parable, Jesus shows different ways in which a servant may respond to a master's absence. What are some of these behaviors? How does the master react to them?

3 Why might the servant in the second parable have taken advantage of his master's absence in the way he did?

4 What do the actions of the bridesmaids tell us about what it means to be "wise" and "foolish"?

5 What is communicated through the image of the closed door in the third parable?

A Guide to the Reading

If participants have not read this section already, read it aloud. Otherwise go on to "Questions for Application."

Jesus uses images of masters and servants frequently in his parables. Whenever we hear a parable introduced with these characters, we can be certain that we will be led to think about issues of stewardship and responsibility.

In the first parable in our session, servants are waiting for their master to return from a wedding. Since it is late at night, the servants' assistance is necessary for the master to enter the house, for the door would have been locked from the inside.

Jesus' listeners would have had quite clearly defined notions of the roles of masters and servants. For that reason, the conclusion of this parable would have come as a shock to their sensibilities. Jesus knew this. He introduces the conclusion with the words *truly I tell you,* a phrase he uses in Luke only when it precedes a startling image or a hard truth. The image of the master serving his slaves is an arresting one. When Jesus washes his disciples' feet at the Last Supper (in the Gospel of John), he makes the same point: life with God is one of intimacy, in which our essential dignity is enhanced by the love of God.

One of the servants in the second parable does not fare so well. He fails to carry out his responsibilities. It is not that he does not know what is expected of him. He does, and this is the point. But he thinks he can avoid paying the price for disobeying his master's wishes. Rather than using what the master has entrusted to him for the good of his fellow servants, he takes advantage of what has been placed in his care. He takes advantage of what God has entrusted to him. Because he is aware of what he was given and what was expected of him, he is punished.

The third parable involves a festival bridal procession. The "bridesmaids"—literally "maidens" or "virgins"—are to accompany the bridegroom and the bride in this procession. The problem is that the groom is for some reason delayed. The maidens wait, their "lamps"—probably torches—burning. Eventually some of the lamps begin to go out. Half of the maidens are prepared with more oil. Half are not, and they must hasten in the middle of the night to find more. By the time they return, it is too late. The groom has returned, the feast has begun, and the door is closed.

The basic meaning of the parable is easy enough to detect. As we have seen before, the meal is a common biblical image for the union of God and humanity. Banquets in particular bring to mind the final gathering of the Lord and his people (Matthew 22:1–14). In addition, Jesus refers to himself as the "bridegroom" elsewhere in Scripture (Matthew 9:15). Virgins bear their own symbolism. They represent lives focused on the Lord's return, in light of which other concerns fade in importance. So it is clear that we have here a parable about the coming final judgment and about how we are to relate to it.

The groom, Jesus lets us know, may be "delayed": he may not come as soon as we expect. In the meantime, we must remain prepared for his return. Note that the issue is not sleep, despite Jesus' final comment on the parable—"Keep awake" (Matthew 25:13)—which probably refers to the entire set of instructions that Jesus has been giving (Matthew 24:1–25:13). In fact, all the maidens do fall asleep while they wait. The problem is not that the maidens allowed themselves to rest but that they were not prepared. The wise virgins were prepared, so they could welcome the groom with confidence.

The wise disciple, then, is prepared for the Lord because she has a sufficient supply of oil that will light her lamp and enable her to see him when he returns. Our oil is faith: trust in the Lord that guards us from needless worry and at the same time equips us for living in the world, sharing the light of God's love. We are not to be anxious—rather, we are to have sufficient store of the faith that helps us see the Lord's presence so that we may recognize and join him when he comes.

Sometimes we are tempted to think that we can make up for lost time later. Jesus challenges us to rethink that assumption.

Questions for Application

40 minutes
Choose questions according to your interest and time.

1 What do you think it means to be "ready" for the Lord's return? What does it mean in terms of your inner life? What does it mean in terms of your practical, everyday living?

2 What makes it difficult for you to keep your focus on the Lord?

3 Describe a time in which the "world" as you knew it (your home, town, job, family, a period in society) came to a sort of end. Were you prepared? Was there any way you could have been better prepared? What does this experience suggest about being prepared to die?

4 Would you prefer to know the exact moment when the world or your life will come to an end? Why or why not?

5 If you did know that you were going to die in a week, how would you live in the intervening days?

6 Jesus suggests that for those who are prepared, the fact of his coming should not be a reason to fear. What factors lead us to fear the end of life, despite Jesus' assurances?

If silence persists, rephrase your question, but resist the temptation to answer it yourself.

Stephen Board, *Great Doctrines of the Bible*

Approach to Prayer

15 minutes
Use this approach—or create your own!

◆ Pray the following prayer together. Then invite group members to share brief, spontaneous prayers expressing their hopes for their own lives in light of Jesus' call to be ready.

We thank you, Lord, for the opportunity to study and pray together over these past weeks. We pray that the seeds that have been sown here will continue to flourish in our lives, drawing us closer to you so that all who encounter us might encounter you through our love and compassion. Work within us and open us to your mercy and to the good news of your love for all people.

Saints in the Making

Do Not Be Careless

This section is a supplement for individual reading.

St. Teresa of Ávila (1515–82) founded a reformed branch of the Carmelite religious order (this reformed group is called the Discalced Carmelites, which means "without shoes," reflecting the strict nature of St. Teresa's reform). She wrote major works on spirituality, as well as poetry. The following is an excerpt from a poem of hers entitled "For the Veiling of Sister Isabel De Los Angeles."

> *So that you will be watchful, Sister,*
> *Today they have veiled you;*
> *On that your Heaven depends;*
> *Do not be careless*
>
> The veil so graceful
> Proclaims you keep vigil,
> The watchful sentinel
> Awaiting her Bridegroom
> Who as the famed thief
> Will come with surprise;
> *Do not be careless . . .*
>
> Keep ready your oil jar
> Of merits and deeds,
> Ample to keep
> Your lamp aflame
> Lest outside you be kept
> When He comes.
> *Do not be careless . . .*
>
> Be constant in care,
> Fulfilling all bravely,
> What you vowed today
> Until death comes,
> In keeping well your watch
> With the Bridegroom you will enter
> *Do not be careless.*

When Will Jesus Return?

We have just read some parables that speak about Jesus' return, the last judgment, and the end of time. The timing of Jesus' return has intrigued Christians since the early days of the Church. Yet though he made it clear that he would indeed return, he made it just as clear that the moment of that return was hidden.

Jesus may have warned us, as he did in the parable of the ten bridesmaids, to be ready for his return at any time, but that has not stopped Christians from trying, in both fear and hope, to predict that moment anyway.

Most of these attempts to forecast the Lord's return have been tied to signs of the end in the Bible given by Jesus himself, by St. Paul, and by the author of the book of Revelation. In the midst of suffering, persecution, war, and what might seem to be the end of the world, at least as we know it, it is understandable that Christians might try to find a scenario of the end in the combination of these signs—and hope for an end to their suffering in connection with the Lord's coming.

In recent history, the words of Catholic mystics and visionaries both approved and unapproved have prompted many to view contemporary events as signs that history is moving toward its culmination. Some other Christians have actually attempted to calculate the exact time of the Lord's return. In 1843, an American religious leader named William Miller declared that he had determined that the Lord would return in that year. One of his associates made several more specific predictions and ultimately decided that the Lord would return on October 22, 1844. This nonevent came to be known by his followers as "The Great Disappointment," and those who gathered with Miller in expectation of the end were the first members of what is today the Seventh-day Adventist Church.

In the last decades of the twentieth century, perhaps inspired by the coming millennium, many Christians, both Protestant and Catholic, developed a keen interest in predicting the sequence of events of the end times and relating this sequence to contemporary events. Schemas were worked and publicized in books and on Internet sites.

What does the Catholic Church say about all of this?

Throughout its history, the Church as a whole has remained mindful of Jesus' teaching, which contains general, symbolic warnings about what the end times may look like but cautions strongly against trying to predict when the events of the end times will occur.

The Church's teaching emphasizes that we need not look for the last days to come at some point in the future, for we are already in the last days, the time inaugurated by Jesus' first coming (Hebrews 1:1–2). With Jesus' death and resurrection we have come into the final period of God's dealings with the human race. These *are* the end times, filled, as they have been for two thousand years, with all of the signs of which Jesus spoke.

The Church teaches that in God's time, all that has been spoken of will be fulfilled: a final struggle of good and evil, God's triumph, Christ's return, our judgment, and the glory of a new heaven and new earth. But when? As the bishops at the Second Vatican Council (1962–65) wrote in *The Pastoral Constitution on the Church in the Modern World:*

We know neither the moment of the consummation of the earth and of man, nor the way in which the universe will be transformed. The form of this world, distorted by sin, is passing away, and we are taught that God is preparing a new dwelling and a new earth in which righteousness dwells, in which happiness will fill and surpass all the desires of peace arising in the hearts of men (section 39).

Until that moment, we are called to live in the way Jesus describes in the parable of the ten bridesmaids: being prepared, using the gift of life wisely, and hoping for the full coming of God's kingdom. Jesus' parables help us to steer clear of two extremes. If we forget that he is indeed coming, we will be tempted to live with no regard to the ultimate meaning and purpose of our lives. On the other hand, if we fixate on the possible moment of that coming, we will be tempted to forget the necessity of living in the present that God has provided and meeting him in that moment, in love and hope.

"Keep awake therefore, for you know neither the day nor the hour" (Matthew 25:13).

Suggestions for Bible Discussion Groups

Like a camping trip, a Bible discussion group works best if you agree on where you're going and how you intend to get there. Many groups use their first meeting to talk over such questions and reach a consensus. Here is a checklist of issues, with bits of advice from people who have experience in Bible discussions. (A planning discussion will go more smoothly if the leaders have thought through the following issues beforehand.)

Agree on your purpose. Are you getting together to gain wisdom and direction for your lives? to finally get acquainted with the Bible? to support one another in following Christ? to encourage those who are exploring—or reexploring—the Church? for other reasons?

Agree on attitudes. For example: "We're all beginners here." "We're here to help one another understand and respond to God's word." "We're not here to offer counseling or direction to one another." "We want to read Scripture prayerfully." What do *you* wish to emphasize? Make it explicit!

Agree on ground rules. Barbara J. Fleischer, in her useful book *Facilitating for Growth,* recommends that a group clearly state its approach to the following:

- ◆ *Preparation.* Do we agree to read the material and prepare the answers to the questions before each meeting?
- ◆ *Attendance.* What kind of priority will we give to our meetings?
- ◆ *Self-revelation.* Are we willing to help the others in the group gradually get to know us—our weaknesses as well as our strengths, our needs as well as our gifts?
- ◆ *Listening.* Will we commit ourselves to listening to one another?
- ◆ *Confidentiality.* Will we keep everything that is shared *with* the group *in* the group?
- ◆ *Discretion.* Will we refrain from sharing about the faults and sins of people who are not in the group?
- ◆ *Encouragement and support.* Will we give as well as receive?
- ◆ *Participation.* Will we give each person the time and opportunity to make a contribution?

You could probably take a pen and draw a circle around *listening* and *confidentiality*. Those two points are especially important.

The following items could be added to Fleischer's list:

◆ *Relationship with parish.* Is our group part of the adult faith-formation program? independent but operating with the express approval of the pastor? not a parish-based group?

◆ *New members.* Will we let new members join us once we have begun the six weeks of discussions?

Agree on housekeeping.

◆ *When will we meet?*

◆ *How often will we meet?* Meeting weekly or every other week is best if you can manage it. William Riley remarks, "Meetings once a month are too distant from each other for the threads of the last session not to be lost" *(The Bible Study Group: An Owner's Manual).*

◆ *How long will meetings run?*

◆ *Where will we meet?*

◆ *Is any setup needed?* Christine Dodd writes that "the problem with meeting in a place like a church hall is that it can be very soul-destroying," given the cold, impersonal feel of many church facilities. If you have to meet in a church facility, Dodd recommends doing something to make the area homey *(Making Scripture Work).*

◆ *Who will host the meetings?* Leaders and hosts are not necessarily the same people.

◆ *Will we have refreshments?* If so, who will provide them?

◆ *What about child care?* Most experienced leaders of Bible discussion groups discourage bringing infants or other children to adult Bible discussions.

Agree on leadership. You need someone to facilitate—to keep the discussion on track, to see that everyone has a chance to speak, to help the group stay on schedule. Rena Duff, editor of the newsletter *Sharing God's Word Today,* recommends having two or three people take turns leading the discussions.

It's okay if the leader is not an expert on the Bible. You have this booklet, and if questions come up that no one can answer, you can delegate a participant to do a little research between meetings. It's important for the leader to set an example of listening, to draw out the quieter members (and occasionally restrain the more vocal ones), to move the group on when it gets stuck, to remind the members of their agreements, and to summarize what the group is accomplishing.

Bible discussion is an opportunity to experience the fulfillment of Jesus' promise "Where two or three are gathered in my name, I am there among them" (Matthew 18:20). Put your discussion group in Jesus' hands. Pray for the guidance of the Spirit. And have a great time exploring God's word together!

Y ou can use this booklet just as well for individual study as for group discussion. While discussing the Bible with other people can be a rich experience, there are advantages to reading on your own. For example:

◆ You can focus on the points that interest you most.

◆ You can go at your own pace.

◆ You can be completely relaxed and unashamedly honest in your answers to all the questions, since you don't have to share them with anyone!

My suggestions for using this booklet on your own are these:

◆ Don't skip the Questions to Begin. The questions can help you as an individual reader warm up to the topic of the reading.

◆ Take your time on the Questions for Careful Reading and Questions for Application. While a group will probably not have enough time to work on all the questions, you can allow yourself the time to consider all of them if you are using the booklet by yourself.

◆ After reading the Guide to the Reading, go back and reread the Scripture text before answering the Questions for Application.

◆ Take the time to look up all the parenthetical Scripture references.

◆ Since you control the pace, give yourself plenty of opportunities to reflect on the meaning of the parables for you. Let your reading be an opportunity for these words to become God's words to you.

Resources

Bibles

The following editions of the Bible contain the full set of biblical books recognized by the Catholic Church, along with a great deal of useful explanatory material:

- ◆ The Catholic Study Bible (Oxford University Press), which uses the text of the New American Bible
- ◆ The Catholic Bible: Personal Study Edition (Oxford University Press), which also uses the text of the New American Bible
- ◆ The New Jerusalem Bible, the regular (not the reader's) edition (Doubleday)

Books

- ◆ Richard N. Longenecker, ed., *The Challenge of Jesus' Parables* (Grand Rapids, Mich.: W. B. Eerdmans, 2000).
- ◆ John R. Donahue, S.J., *The Gospel in Parable: Metaphor, Narrative, and Theology in the Synoptic Gospels* (Philadelphia: Fortress Press, 1988).
- ◆ Robert Farrar Capon, *Kingdom, Grace, Judgment: Paradox, Outrage, and Vindication in the Parables of Jesus* (Grand Rapids, Mich.: W. B. Eerdmans, 2001).
- ◆ Arland J. Hultgren, *The Parables of Jesus: A Commentary* (Grand Rapids, Mich.: W. B. Eerdmans, 2000).
- ◆ Wilfrid J. Harrington, O.P., *Parables Told by Jesus: A Contemporary Approach to the Parables* (New York: Alba House, 1974).
- ◆ Kenneth E. Bailey, *Poet and Peasant, and Through Peasant Eyes: A Literary-Cultural Approach to the Parables in Luke* (Grand Rapids, Mich.: W. B. Eerdmans, 1983).

How has Scripture had an impact on your life? Was this booklet helpful to you in your study of the Bible? Please send comments, suggestions, and personal experiences to Kevin Perrotta, General Editor, Trade Editorial Department, Loyola Press, 3441 N. Ashland Ave., Chicago, IL 60657.